"When we arrive at [the] wise friend has stoo[ped] to handle the illusio[ns]  tions we raise, the aging we endure, and the ordinary ravishments of daily life we may have forgotten but now cherish again. And all along, it turns out, the God of wise love has been holding onto us. Because we are his, and he, by his lavish grace, is ours. These poems offer a kind of wisdom-formation in Christ, filling our days with tasted truth and sturdy hope."

—**Zack Eswine**, author of *Recovering Eden: The Gospel according to Ecclesiastes*

"Susan Erikson's well-crafted free verse beautifully covers the thematic terrain of the entire book of Ecclesiastes. The oral and mnemonic power of poetry takes center stage in free verse because it resembles ordinary speech, but artfully condenses language and seasons it with internal cadence and rhyme. This fine poetry should be a significant aid to Bible study."

—**Gregory Edward Reynolds**, pastor emeritus, Amoskeag Presbyterian Church

"It is rare to find a book of poetry that touches the soul so deeply that it serves as both a great work of art and as a devotional. Yet that is exactly what Susan Erikson's *Bones in the Womb* achieves. A uniquely immersive journey into Ecclesiastes, Susan carries her reader through the 'cry of the heart' and into the arms of the only one in whom we have our hope and rescue: our Heavenly Father. This book is a treasure trove of depth and encouragement and a must-read for all."

—**Sarah Dudley**, Children's Church teacher

"*Bones in the Womb* provides a twenty-first-century perspective on the themes of Ecclesiastes. I found the poems to faithfully apply the Preacher's vision to the modern world. I found myself, bound to an imperfect body in an imperfect world, still desiring to hear the good news of the gospel and the joy that only the indwelling of the Holy Spirit brings to each day."

—**Mark Fink**, veterinarian

"We may not view our lives as being full of futile pursuits, but Susan Erikson's poetry prompts the reader to reflect on what we observe today that can frustrate and fail to satisfy. She brings a New Testament framing of Solomon's book of wisdom with biblical allusion and a descriptive look at man's ageless pursuits that encompass the deeply upsetting and truly beautiful. While thorough in relating life's modern-day experiences, there is a Psalm-like hopefulness and expressive acknowledgement of God."

—**Kingsley Elder**, follower of Christ

# Bones in the Womb

# Bones in the Womb

*Living by Faith in an Ecclesiastes World*

Susan E. Erikson

RESOURCE *Publications* · Eugene, Oregon

BONES IN THE WOMB
Living by Faith in an Ecclesiastes World

Copyright © 2024 Susan E. Erikson. All rights reserved. Except for brief quotations in critical publications or reviews, no part of this book may be reproduced in any manner without prior written permission from the publisher. Write: Permissions, Wipf and Stock Publishers, 199 W. 8th Ave., Suite 3, Eugene, OR 97401.

Resource Publications
An Imprint of Wipf and Stock Publishers
199 W. 8th Ave., Suite 3
Eugene, OR 97401

www.wipfandstock.com

PAPERBACK ISBN: 979-8-3852-1274-3
HARDCOVER ISBN: 979-8-3852-1275-0
EBOOK ISBN: 979-8-3852-1276-7

VERSION NUMBER 04/30/24

Scripture quotations are from The ESV® Bible (The Holy Bible, English Standard Version®), © 2001 by Crossway, a publishing ministry of Good News Publishers. Used by permission. All rights reserved.

This book is dedicated to every pilgrim on the road between this flawed world and the world to come. The way is often steep, the living is difficult and messy. Such is Christ's Church, this side of heaven. Keep walking. Meditate on the Word. Fear God. Stay focused. Only Christ will satisfy. And His promises are truly Yes! And Amen!

# Introduction

Western culture is a universe of a thousand distractions all vying for our attention and loyalty. It is a world of excessive access, with a constant supply of potential experiences primarily focused on the self, more than anything else. Yet nothing satisfies. The *Preacher* of Ecclesiastes would understand. The overarching themes of Ecclesiastes: the human desire to chase after this world's empty dreams and promises for personal satisfaction, the inevitability of death, and man's existential need for God, make these themes particularly poignant given the core messages of the twenty-first century. We are gods, we tell each other, with the power to manipulate any corner of creation; whether daily weather, or our own bodies. We expend enormous energy and funds trying to cheat death. We relentlessly pursue science and medicine, we talk at length about "being safe," and we have decided we do not require God. We are experts at chasing after the wind. We are also a people of great despair and loneliness.

Christians are not immune to this worldview. A sizable number of us now consider the little computer we carry in our back pockets to be an extension of us. It is also the access point to the noisy world clamoring for our attention. We of the twenty-first century need to hear what the *Preacher* has to say. We need to recognize our desire for what does not satisfy. We need to realize how much this life will always be a struggle between those desires and weaknesses, and God's hope, and that it is necessary to face our desires head-on with the Word of God. We need to encourage ourselves and each other that resting in faith in His promises, and obedience to

His commands make all the difference. This message is extremely counter-cultural, rubbing against all the habits and experiences of our lives: our streaming services; social media; the siren bill boards along the highways tempting us to fulfill all our cravings; the music cascading through our heads; and all too often the normal daily (and hourly) news; full of fear and darkness.

I have been intrigued for years by Ecclesiastes; its honesty about human struggles, its frank expose of the futility of our excursions into stuff and experiences for meaning and satisfaction; its persistent reminder that death is on everyone's bucket list; and the correct recourse for human peace in the face of this world, is a relationship with the God of heaven. Nothing sentimental here, but the best place for every believer to start.

Most companion books on Ecclesiastes, whether prose or poetry, move from verse to verse. I have chosen a different route. The poems in this volume are a response to the overall text. I have focused on the following themes: Chasing After the Wind; A Time to Die; Fear God; and A Pleasing Aroma. And from each theme, I am constantly reminded that the twenty-first century is an Ecclesiastes world, a world that needs clarity and truth, and a way back out of the chaos and despair that would define us all.

# Contents

## Prologue

Bones in the Womb | 2
Keeping Watch by Night | 3
Babbling | 4
That Passing Moment of Clarity | 6

## Chasing After the Wind

All is Vapor | 8
Fantasies | 10
Reconstruction | 12
Time | 13
Better Than Folly | 14
Panoply of the Dull | 16
Blinders | 18
Betrayal | 20
This World's Complaint | 21
Lost | 23
A Religious Experiment | 25
The Bard | 26
The Cry of the Heart | 28
For a Week or Two | 30
War | 32
Conflict | 34
The Daily Battle | 36
An Unhappy Business | 38
Passing By | 40

Utopian Dreams | 42
No Legacy | 43
They Cannot See | 45
Looking for Justice | 46
Hubris | 48
Talking Heads | 49
Solutions | 51
Ozymandias Still Speaks | 53
God Gave Them Up | 55
Lament for the Desolation of Man | 56
On the Phone | 57
Prone to Wander | 59

## A Time to Die

Adamah | 62
Called to Die | 64
Hard Truth | 66
Grief | 68
Numbering | 69
The Sting | 70
The Last Campaign | 72
Body and Soul | 73
Grief Comes | 75
Separation | 76
Life's Bites | 77
First to Last | 79
In Honor of Nelson | 80

## Fear God

Lost and Wandering | 82
A Fork in the Road | 84
Let Me Hide Myself in Thee | 88
The Wonder of the Cross | 90
Under the Blood | 93

Rebuttal | 94
Holy Food | 96
Fidget | 98
Promises | 101
This is the Day | 103
Rough Seas | 105
Sacred Guardians | 107
Letting Go | 109
Discerning Grace | 111
To My Granddaughter | 113
The Last Battle | 114
The Latest Race | 116
A Soliloquy of Faith | 118
Resting | 119
I Am Unraveled | 120
Providence | 121
Last Days | 124
God With Us | 126

## A Pleasing Aroma

I Didn't Know How Hungry I Was | 132
A Pleasing Aroma | 133
Who But God | 135
And Then They Sang | 137
Sight Unseen | 139
Stones Speak | 140
God's Re-creation | 142
The Tall Man | 143
Rescue | 145
One Night | 147
My Soul Waits for the LORD | 150
Final Thoughts | 154

# Prologue

## Bones in the Womb

Here we are,
Bones in the womb.
The elements
that could have
built great wisdom,
Doomed.
Lives full of promise,
Much preferring
pacts with rebels,
Liking too much,
Grand autonomy
at any cost.
It is a loss,
A taste for tragedy,
That swiftly leads
to building hell,
And draws us,
Wearily,
Into the tomb.

## Keeping Watch by Night

Why do they despise the shepherds,
Those who raise the lambs
to take away their sin?
Is it association with man's weaker parts,
The awful truth,
They need the shepherds
and their work?
They need these dirty,
Rough,
And vulgar men
to bring the lambs,
The lambs to cleanse their dirt,
To cleanse all rough and vulgar souls.
The blood,
The sacrifice,
Can rend and rip at wretched hearts,
But there is also order
with the priests,
And proper ritual
that can make distance,
Make religion tamer,
More acceptable,
Less fiercely confrontational with sin.
The shepherds bear the dirt
before the lambs bear dirty hearts.
And in that weary transfer,
They who shepherded redemption in the field,
Remind us all that gross iniquity has been revealed.

# Babbling

Once people tried
to build a mountain
close enough
to touch God's face
and never die.
God turned their language
into cluttered air,
Misunderstanding
codified from mouth to ear.
No words to speak,
No unity,
The only grand epiphany
was what could not be shared.
And so the crowd
dispersed,
Moved on.

It could be worse.

One day
the people tried again.
This time the mountain
came to them,
A ziggurat of words
that captured energy and waves
to recreate a passing thought.
A momentary lapse of judgment,
Suddenly released
to forty million listeners,

From mouth to ear.
Too fast
for contemplation,
Grand impulsiveness
in milliseconds everywhere.
And wisdom
hardly ever touched
a dangling participle,
Subject–verb alignment,
Context,
Content,
Reasoning,
Or comprehension.
Language here—
It looked the same.
No trouble
recognizing every word.
But certainly, no understanding.
Only cluttered air
and vacuous wind.
No unity.
And so the crowd,
In tribal groups
that complemented their despair,
Dispersed,
Moved on.

It could be worse.

## That Passing Moment of Clarity

Some days,
The sin rolls in like fog.
It touches everything,
Like smoke from cigarettes,
Malodorous odors
clinging hard to heart and mind.
It leaves a bad taste in my mouth.
And once again
I am most visibly aware
of just how terrible,
How miserable
and monstrous,
Is that part of me that loves the dark,
That part that stains my every action, every thought.
I hate it.

# Chasing After the Wind

## All is Vapor

People come,
People go,
From light of dawn
to glowing dusk,
The days roll on
and on and on.
Whether harmony
or wars increase,
The boy is young,
The man grows old,
Yet earth remains,
Seedtime, harvest,
Heat and cold,
Summer and winter,
Day and night
shall never cease.

Ideas blow south,
Dreams blow north,
Brilliant schemes
ride winds around and
around and around.
Wherever thoughts and reasons fly,
Wisdom seems to pass man by.
Each time we hope
for better words,
Or steadier hands.
What has been done,
Was done before.

The world grinds on.
It cannot capture steady peace.
There's nothing new.
Yet earth remains,
Seedtime, harvest,
Heat and cold,
Summer and winter,
Day and night
shall never cease.

## Fantasies

We would be wizards,
Weaving,
Spinning,
Conjuring up ultimates.
We capture stars
and fling them back to earth,
Where harnessed,
Golden energy
will someday resurrect the soul,
Imaginations only grasp still higher,
Ever higher.
Towers of straining,
Hubris reaching up to capture heaven's floor.

I say to you,
There's nothing new.
It's all been done before.
This should be sung,
Recited,
Every word recounted,
Known.
But we are not rememberers.

We see ourselves as giants,
Grand immortals,
Bards of glory,
Thinking our own story
is the most unique,

The dream most likely
to succeed.

Where are the archivists
who chant forgotten memories?
Who savor all things old
and trade in vast collections
of what modern man considers dull inanities,
Or maybe only myths?
From these,
Observant chroniclers have chosen items
just because they hold
the most extravagantly precious Truth,
Veracity that comprehends
and undergirds all history,
All human lore
from dusty, ancient texts,
To bureaucratic scrolls and notes
on military routs,
To boasting conquerors in cuneiform.
And so I say to you again,
There's nothing new.
It's all been done before.

# Reconstruction

We would be deities,
Recreating sacred out of self.
Recreating selves
by adding on and taking off
the parts that do not please.
We have become,
In these,
The ancient gods,
Who formed the man and woman
out of broken pieces,
Leftovers,
To mold their fantasies.

# Time

Time eats time,
A mouth that swallows memory,
A mind that toils on and on,
Beyond
where man has ever been,
To where no man has ever known,
A constant folding of our words,
Our thoughts,
Our actions,
All to dust.
Such fragile matter,
Old,
Reused,
Applied and honed
to marry eager flesh
with bone.
And like the wind,
That always flows
and flings on past,
Our time gets eaten up
from first to last.

## Better Than Folly

We like to see our wisdom
dressed impressively,
A brash,
Celebrity of words
and actions,
Someone we could worship.
*How profound!*
We say,
Nodding to each other.
*Surely we have chosen well*
*by following*
*this fellow's grand pronouncements.*
*Who cares what promises will spoil*
*or decay.*
*Today is for today,*
*And just by listening we have been made a*
*more enlightened group,*
*Surely more in tune with each and every truth,*
*Your truth and mine,*
*Than what we first heard shouted,*
*Argued in a balanced and wide-ranging topical discussion*
*yesterday.*
Beware.
Wisdom may not be so loud.
Wisdom doesn't cater to seduction,
Or destruction,
Doesn't barter with the truth.
Wisdom may come quietly,
Behind the scenes,

A word of hope and promises,
Of life unfolding
from a poor man's mouth.
When Holy Wisdom
travels up and down the ordinary streets,
She searches depth,
She forages for honesty,
She calls out in the market,
Seeking bright sagacity in busy places,
City gates.
*Where are the wise who fear the* LORD,
She asks,
*Who diligently pursue good counsel*
*and accept reproof?*
*Where are the whisperers of faith,*
*The gentle answers*
*sharpening in strength*
*by turning hearts away from wrath?*
*Where are the people humbled by the* LORD
*in Word and deed?*
*I hear the lies,*
*I see the foolish everywhere,*
*Where are the wise?*

## Panoply of the Dull

Everything,
*Through the Lens,*
Is what our culture contemplates.
Whatever's new,
Whatever satisfies our angst
for being best,
For looking better than the rest,
Is suddenly declared
the World of True.
And every conversation,
Every media displayed,
Every attitude and use of words
must each be funneled through
that *Lens,*
Must fit the groove,
Or be forever ostracized,
Despised,
Dismantled,
Undermined.
The *Lens* dictates our every move.
No room for other views,
And no creative soul,
No whimsical array
of plot and irony,
But only spirit-crushing,
Dull rebranding
of another's work,
To make what doesn't fit,
Conform.

Such work is only flimsy paper,
Flatness masquerading as an art,
But only overwhelming bland and toneless,
Dry monotony,
That does not even know,
Or understand
the bright vocabulary necessary
to exult in fire,
Or the grand imagination
for a heart to revive the brash,
Or lift a phoenix rising from the ash.

# Blinders

One woman on the street,
Can rightly name
the folks and circumstance
that left her
wrapped in ragged blankets,
Sitting on discarded chairs,
But cannot see
the circumstances of her ragged soul
that keeps her there.

One man
is still a boy
because of drugs
and careless raising.
Something in his life
is always going wrong,
And he is sure
it could be fixed if only ...
(Here he names a list of possibilities
that change from day to day.)
If only he could see
that he is also keeping life from moving on,
And peace is always
just beyond his reach.

He has always had advantages:
The finer schools,
The opportunities that promise jobs,
Advancement far beyond the ordinary crowd.

And he believes he has it all.

Then why is there unruly discontent,
A hard despair
that hides beneath his skin,
And fills his pores with acrimony?
He can point a finger everywhere,
But toward himself.
And his own heart
can barely bear the pain.

She came from ordinary circumstances,
The kind of middle-class existence
that can organize
a sense of right and wrong,
That frames morality
on up-to-date and cultural preferences.
Good at noticing
when others fail to meet her expectations.
Not as easily adroit
at recognizing
her appalling faults.

So easy to discover
other peoples' sins,
And judge our lesser neighbors
by their weakest points.
So ugly to see personal guilt
as indiscretions,
Minor defects,
Not as serious flaws
for which Another's life was crushed,
Poured out like water,
All His bones made out of joint.

## Betrayal

He makes me sad,
Digging through the layers of his life—
The Cenozoic,
Then the Mesozoic—
We keep digging.
Gradations of his broken promises.
This is the level we find artifacts—
Pawn shop tickets,
Papers never signed,
Discarded trash
that follows careless habits,
All the mess he left behind
for us to find,
To understand at last,
That he had only built illusion's dream,
A paradise of his invention,
Somehow hoping
saying it aloud would make it real,
Telling us a story
(words already shredding in the wind)
would make him feel alive,
Make us believe.
Instead,
We stand here sorting through the wreckage,
Finding he was only ghost,
A tenuous hold on truth,
And gifted most to lie and steal.

## This World's Complaint

Some days,
I feel like I am
anchored hard to earth,
The weight of my own feet
are merely dragging dirt,
And gravity has pulled me down.
*That's this world,*
I say,
As I keep struggling in pain.

Some nights,
It's difficult to sleep,
As accusations in my mind
keep dredging deeply
into buried thoughts,
So easily ignored by day,
But in the dark,
I cannot make them go away.
*That's this world,*
I say,
While life's unfinished business
clutters up my tired brain.

This world!
This world
is all about the clicks,
About how many people notice me,
How much I can accomplish,
While presenting my identity,

My perfect self,
My most authentic version
of reality.

This world!
This world
is swallowing my energies,
Is creeping
into all the crevices
I had set aside for rest and peace,
And filling them
with clamoring anxieties.
How can I exit off
this endless hamster wheel?
Where everything I think and do,
Is undermined by who
I really am?
There is no perfect face.
For underneath my perfect page
is only me.
And life,
The life you see,
Is only scam.

# Lost

This world invests in chaos,
Claiming struggle rules.
*Accept it!*
*Grow and go within it!*
*Find embrace*
*in all the stumbling that stings,*
The sages say.
*Living with distraught,*
*With upside down,*
*Makes greater art,*
The Tempter adds,
*A richer comprehension of delight.*
*Dissembling truth*
*is honesty*
*and authenticity.*
But what is left?
Despair,
Discouragement,
A wandering mind
that trembles in the dark,
A keening heart
that wallows in the things
that breaks a soul apart.
And stumbling,
Such exotic stumbling
that fractures peace,
Can never reach the something
every seeker
truly wants to know.

The soul,
Instead,
Is lost,
And leaves a disembodied life,
A broken heart.

## A Religious Experiment

They're gathering together,
Change-makers,
Thinkers,
Activists.
*We all are one,*
They say.
*With greater hopes of making here*
*a more inclusive world,*
*More durable,*
*And more diverse,*
*Where we can all be unified,*
*No matter what or who we are,*
*As long as we are on one side.*
They're reaching
for a welcoming,
Affirming,
Safer space.
The list of sinners
sanctified,
Is matched
with present theological displays.
They want it to work well.
They're seeking a more sacred place.
No others need apply.
This is a yearning
for a church
without a Christ.
And trying
to make heaven out of earth,
Will always lead to hell.

## The Bard

He makes money off sin,
And the words that he sings
reveal
just what has been
festering,
Smoldering
deep in his bones,
How the ragged desire
to find a good home,
A place meant to fit
one who lives by his gut,
By the passions that swallow up
moments,
And cut into hard daily quarrels
that crumple his soul.
They leave their own scars,
From the clubs to the bars,
A bard of distinction,
A grand storyteller,
A singer of truth,
Yet he keeps a limp hold
on his endless delights,
Making room,
Always room for whatever ignites,
Always captured by guilt.
And it's written
all over his ragged face,

From the ridges
that sculpt
his internal pains,
To his eyes,
Like deep fathoms,
Where darkness remains.
To a fault,
Never free.
For he knows just how weak
and how raw
can a sinful man be.

## The Cry of the Heart

He thought
his truth,
His very own,
Exalted,
Existential truth,
Could save him,
As the weight of pain,
Of disabilities
encroaching miserably,
On every corner of his life,
Began to conquer,
Even paralyze
the breath of hope.
Wealth and name,
And all it gave him,
Looked each morning more like dust
than any sweet commodity,
While all his energies,
Determination,
Any gain,
Was being erased in grand futility.
Resilience paused.
Optimism sighed.
And alcohol,
Revised from previous hopes,
No longer gave a buzz.

It was
a dark and dreadful recognition
of the life
he could not keep.
His work and fame,
Incapable of bringing any soul relief.

## For a Week or Two

I'm driving by
the Christmas lights,
Spectacular,
Fantastical,
And glowing in the shivering night,
With all the bright
inflatables
that decorate a lawn.
I think,
How gaudy!
How unfathomable
I didn't notice this before.
It is as if
the world could conjure
magic,
For a week or two.
And we are able to sustain
the culture's present virtues,
Pause from struggles
for a week or two.
Religiously,
We hope
that this thin wave of weightless celebration
of ourselves,
And our ability to decorate
with plastic and electric lights,

Could possibly deny
the threats of holocaust,
Pandemics,
And the general unhappiness
which borders on despair,
At least,
Could hold their possibility at bay
for just this week,
Or for a week or two.
*Just two weeks, please,*
We say,
*To make some space*
*for personal enjoyment,*
*And a sense of peace*
*that carries weight.*
*A grand chimera, please,*
*Just one more day,*
*So we can all pretend*
*it's always been this way.*

# War

The fight
for one man's soul
is raging in the heavens.
Earth would drag him
down to dust.
Sin would grind his spirit,
Crush him
with its weight.

The saints,
Meanwhile,
Are praying,
Pleading here before
the gate of heaven's sacred throne.

And still the serpent taunts
at any thoughts of clarity,
Any passing seconds of a raw humility,
Where personal guilt is seen
so clearly,
Seen so painfully.
What might have been
a moment of sagacity
is undermined,
Is drowned in whisperings of shame and doubt,
The sudden need for hiding—
Don't reveal too much.
Don't let them see me as I truly am.

The prayers go on and on,
A sacred incense rising up,
A fragrant offering.
LORD,
*Bow your ear to our prayer,*
They cry.
And bend their hearts before Him,
Naming this man to their Savior's care.
*Not our will but yours.*

For now,
He'd rather be a grifter
peddling scam,
Than face the LORD
who rules the universe,
Who offers peace the man could never earn,
Or ever will deserve.
He'd rather steal the gift,
Keep the sin,
And work redemption out himself.
And Satan,
Going to and fro upon the earth
is glad to hear.

# Conflict

I am watching
what this world calls
entertainment—
Plot,
Explosive exposition full of fury,
Climax,
Denouement—
But all the parts
are full of shadows,
Antiheroes,
Choosing dark to overcome,
Like all the other fallen gods
of ancient days.
No honor here,
No love of truth and light,
No victory securely won.
The stories
craving hard on coveting,
And ruthless acts,
Less on grace.
More on saving
by inviting evil's hand
in work,
To bolster strength.
It shows a Man most base.
No justice here,
No beauty,
No known possibility to end despair.

It's what we wear.
No hope that what would crush us
has already been undone.

Where are the heroes?
Send me heroes!
Not this dance
with death and sin.
It seems that we've been standing
in the shadows
for so long,
We cannot even see the dark
eclipsing everything that speaks of Right,
And in our lostness,
Eagerly let all that is unholy in.

## The Daily Battle

Everyday,
My walk with God seems sparce,
Too quiet on His part,
And I am more distracted from
a world of spiritual things,
Toward worlds
not flooded with His harmony.

The dread of man
is conquering peace
with violence.

Everyday.

News in this hypersonic age moves fast,
And bulletins,
Like bullets,
Pass me constantly.
Their noisy sounds repeat
the envies and resentments festering inside
too many souls.
Such harrying
keeps echoing across a precipice of fear and anger,
Virtue bristling with righteous indignation,
Ardent victims flinging wayward hearts into the dark,
And then they die.
It's all despair.
I can't go there.

This earth is all distractions,
A constant repetition of deceits,
All meant to trouble me,
To feast my eyes upon myself,
To make me hesitate,
Accept a meager bit of grace,
Instead of Jesus' bountiful supply.

## An Unhappy Business

Fill up the crevices,
The corners,
Every single square of space
with mad activity,
With doing.
Keep a constant flow.
Don't rest.
Don't stop to think,
To ponder
why the race is not intended
for the swift,
And why the
only way to take a break,
Is if you're sick.

So difficult to unwind
all the winding of my day.
It leaks into my night,
Where even dark cannot dispel
the whirring
thoughts conferring,
Some connecting,
Others disconnecting,
Ideas galloping,
Discussions resurrecting doubts,
What should have remained buried,
Now replayed.

What benefit is doing,
If the doings never cease?
Peace, peace.
I want it in my heart and head.
There is no peace.

## Passing By

We're watching
our own culture
crumbling,
Fracturing
into a thousand fleeting shards—
A wafting, vast decay of fragrances,
Some lost aromas of integrity,
Passing perfumes of responsibility
and honor,
Obscure bouquets,
All shifting,
Fading,
Disintegrating,
Ephemerals
all trying very hard
to smell like Truth.
But there is none.
Its very elemental essence
is already gone.
No whiff of universal guidelines here,
No pungency of power and authority
to back
what once was
far more easily identified
and known as Real.

No reason to reveal
what can't be recognized,
When there is nothing left of Truth
but rotting wind.
*Did you catch that?*
*What is that smell?*
No need to wonder what or why.
*Never mind.*
It is the corpse of our own culture
drifting by.

## Utopian Dreams

Our hearts are light.
This time it will be different.
We are right,
Of course,
Although we cannot see
what lies ahead.
So sure
of our own machinations,
Our inventions.
Time to hurry forward.
This time,
This year,
This project carries dreams,
We think,
Not noting stars
are not aligned for miracles,
When human minds
and hands,
Are making work
outside of heaven's plans.

## No Legacy

When I would wander
through my neighborhood,
There was a flower garden
filling up one corner,
Flush with wild exuberance,
With roses crowding every place,
A blushing mass of beautiful,
Resplendent,
Overcoming space.
I often stopped
to just enjoy it all,
To stand there,
Reveling
in what a gifted gardener could do.
Behind this fragrant feast,
(Almost invisible,
As though an afterthought,
Is there a house?)
A fading edifice
leaned back against the fence,
Exhausted by the view,
A perfect backdrop
for this other-worldly,
But somehow,
Still stark, suburban plot.

One day the owner died,
The gardener gone.
And someone new moved in
to redirect attention to
the dull brown house,
The sagging roof,
And bring its ordinary presence back.
The roses withered
down to twigs,
Exposing graying gravel,
Dirt,
Tufts of errant grass,
And little vacant holes
where glories used to be.
Where once was reckless love,
Surging,
Breathing life,
Now and forever
would be loss,
A sad,
Neglected,
Seedy corner on a quiet street.
What vanity is this,
That makes artistic joy
from living things,
The generous toil of a hand and heart,
Become a weary,
Passing thing,
Forgotten once it meets with death?
No legacy.
And we are left
bereft.

## They Cannot See

They see Creation,
But they don't see God.
How sad
to only see
the image of themselves displayed,
To only hear
the echo of their thoughts.
*If only me,*
They seem to murmur most approvingly,
And miss the wonders staring back—
The rustling leaves,
The restless puffs of clouds that clutter up the sky,
The soaring hawk or darting bees,
(How do they fly?)
The grass and weeds
eternally meandering
through cracks and crevices,
A running squirrel,
A rabbit statue
hoping to be missed
as busy people chatter by.

It must be sin.
What else could make a person blind
to Whom is breathing,
Shouting,
Flashing colors in the wind?

# Looking for Justice

*He will come to judge*
*the world*
*in righteousness and truth.*
That's what we want,
Not judge it based on your belief,
Here neatly juxtaposed by mine.
Not judge it on
all those who hold the reins,
At this moment
here in time.

So many wrongs to right,
So many suffering
from foolishness,
From blind ambition
pampered in its arrogance.
Tyrant virtues
lavishly dispensed,
Calculating,
Cold coercion.
*We've always known*
*what's best for you.*
No grace.
No mercy tempering such hardened force.
Always building up another edifice,
Another towering ziggurat
to coming Eden,

Right around the corner,
Any day now,
All we need is one more rule,
Just one more sacrifice,
Just one more program left
to usher in
our own,
Most glorious,
Eternity.

And yet no justice here.
No Truth.
No Righteousness.
Just misery.

## Hubris

There was a dream
that I could resurrect and rename everything,
Could render nameless naming
into burning through the will and heart,
Could bend a soul
with my own wild imaginations,
Making better worlds
more free.
It would be him,
Or her,
Or they
who overcomes.
I called it good.
But I am only hunger,
Wasting,
Fire,
Swallowing the earth with vanities,
Sculptors of erratic shadows,
Shapers of unmelting,
Melting wax.
I am a Frankenstein of sighs,
Of ancient lies,
Inventing harsh disharmony,
A bleak amorphic misery.
All life has fled.
My petty god is dead.

## Talking Heads

Constant chatter fills the air—
Today's almighty sin exposed.
What is the talking point?
What do we need to say,
To argue,
Sound productively engaged and caring?
*Absolutely shocked.*
*Appalled*
*Can't possibly imagine*
*anyone*
*would think this way.*

Uninterested in sacred wisdom,
Sensing nuisance
in the Holy Writ,
(That need to rein our
own opinions in.)
They rush to be the expert,
Love to make commotion,
Sure that they are gods,
But gods of what?
Gods of running with this Tuesday's crime,
Or Friday's glorious mistake,
Or someone's slip,
A single word or phrase that magnifies his guilt.
See news at eight.

Gods of misery,
Gods that love divisiveness,
That revel in the hope of constant crisis
overflowing life.
But they are dust.
They speak from vacant hearts.
They are not sages,
Simply talking heads,
A passing storm,
Dead and dry solutions
blowing past us,
Echoes in
their own expansive wind.

## Solutions

Thorns and thistles here,
Already multiplying,
Filling every space
with pain and grief,
While those around me
try to plant the Garden
once again.
It can't be done.

I know utopia,
All shimmering
and vacant visions,
Shattered dreams,
But still they plant.
*This time,*
They say,
*It will be different.*
*Somehow,*
*We will overcome*
*the curse.*

The curse is in the hand,
The heart,
The dirt.
It cannot end
without the Bleed.

It does not bend to us,
It does not cater
to our vanity.
It is not Eden
that will satisfy the hurt,
But New Creation
that we need.

## Ozymandias Still Speaks

You'd think,
This world was formed
by gods and kings,
Our works,
A grand memorial
to all our better things,
And we,
Who stand right now,
(Pick any century),
Are giants on the pinnacle
of history.

You would be wrong.
We are instead,
A confluence
of fractured better judgments,
Intellect and insight
swamped by hubris,
Avarice,
That sense that we deserve the adulation,
Heaping praises on our heads.
But we,
Who know so much,
Are only gluttons
of ourselves,
And our pathologies.

We think we represent the light,
The way out from the dark
of lesser days.
We cannot see,
That what goes up,
Too soon comes down
by our own hand,
As ego shakes,
And empties out our glories,
Turns our marvels
into sinking sand,
A heap of shambles,
Buried with our gifts to Man,
To settle in the dust,
Like all the other thousands
scattered here,
Among the dead.

## God Gave Them Up

Grieve,
Grieve the passing
of such grace,
That held this aching world in place.
We did not see
Your hand was there,
Until You lifted it,
And left us
to our hate and our despair.
You left us to ourselves.
What more horrific wrath
is cast
when we unlock our terrible imaginations,
Mold our cruelties,
And pour them out
by our own hands?
What greater judgment
is there still to come
to those who do not fear the Lord?

## Lament for the Desolation of Man

Only flat plateaus,
Only wind and shifting sands,
Dull fragments of forgotten life,
A scattered,
Tipsy line of rubble
winding up and down
an undulating old embankment,
Lost and fading memories in scrubby ground.
Who would have known
a wall stood here?
A barricade of polished stones
that spread for miles and miles,
A sturdy barrier,
Security
against a mad barrage of warrior ego,
Stout and ready to defend
against a fusillade
of rabid horsemen,
Slashing,
Battling footmen
and their archers,
Barbarism dancing furiously with honor,
Executing someone else's sin.
Here lies
the artifacts of pride
in all its cold atrocities—
Blackened,
Blistered piles of rocks
and fields of bones.

## On the Phone

What will they say,
The ones who find
the crumpled heaps of steel and stone
that once was us.

Will lifeless cell phones,
All their chatter gone
to whispers on the wind,
(Artifacts of glass and metal),
Even hint at our idolatry for information
and devotion to ourselves,
A piteous,
Wretched,
Squandering of our own wherewithal.
Will this be clear at all,
Or will the million upon million
wafers of our hubris,
Only mystify
survivors of our fall?

Like archeologists,
In search of carvings,
Cuneiform on clay,
Will they seek books,
Or periodicals,
Or find there's very little evidence
of any meaningful discussions,

Just those random flat, black pads,
Those metal tablets,
Scattered everywhere
like hard confetti
spread across our culture's tomb,
Shiny objects on the street,
They must mean something?
Here and there among the building dust,
Their presence fast becoming fading blur.
And one day,
Strangers seeking out our monuments,
Or passing through,
Will stumble upon remnants
of our greatness,
Long time past,
And wonder who and what we were.

## Prone to Wander

The wind blows by me,
Sweeping up a pile of broken leaves,
Creating paths
for my distracted heart.
And I would follow,
Far more easily,
This breath of God
than Him alone.

My television calls to me.
There may be news,
Or something streaming
to attract my soul.
I could be hearing words of grace,
Yet I abjure,
So easily seduced
by earthly chatter,
Nuanced arguments of nothing,
Opinions tethered to this day.
They guarantee
there will be something scarier
tomorrow,
Far more worrisome,
More stressful
than the quiet contemplation
waiting in His Word,
Waiting to de-stress my agitation,

Promising encouragement,
While raising up indictments
on my skittery soul.
Sharper than a two-edge sword,
But oh, so good
at raising up the dead,
And melting weary hearts of stone.

I have a Martha moment,
Noticing the piles of papers,
All the dust,
The entropy of humanness
that clutters every corner of my life.
So hard to hear
that still small voice
that binds my story into His.
My heart is strife
instead of peace,
And only His relief
can overwhelm my desperate need
to take control,
And bring much needed order
on this tense and tired soul.
There is a restlessness
I cannot fix.
Why do I try,
When greater grace and wisdom
gently
beckons me
to lay it all again before His throne?

# A Time to Die

## Adamah

Here I am,
Close to the ground again.
O Lord,
I seek Your face.
You know I am a fearful person,
Trudging through a frightening world,
A universe,
Whose existential drift
is tampering with sacred things,
Is blurring Your realities,
Creating categories out of wind,
Attempting to install
its own imaginations,
As if an Eden can be made
from quarreling and wax,
From severed truth
detached and shaped
to recreate old lies.
With all our tries,
We have not resurrected life,
But rendered patched-up schemes.
And death is our inheritance.
I look around,
I want to scream,
*Death! It's death!*
Death in everything,
In all I see,
The mad,

The uncreating,
Cleaving,
And undoing of all Beautiful,
To build what's wretched
out of crude,
Destructive dreams.
Forgive us, Lord,
Forgive our vanity.
Without Your breath
we are undone, unmade.
Without Your hands to hold us up,
We only trade our troubles
for a rabbit hole
of hopeful wishes.
Lord, we hurt.
We have forgotten
we were born from dust,
And into dust we shall return.
Our self-exalting aggrandizements,
All our boastful science
giving birth,
We are not grand Prometheans.
Surely, we have always been,
And ever more shall be
just dirt.

## Called to Die

We are all witnesses.
When those once strong are bent
to face the grave at last,
Our hearts,
All bending down with them,
Cry out.
We are undone.
For all will be consigned
one day,
To dust.
It does not matter whether good or bad.
The soldier hiding in the trench,
The preacher exegeting Truth,
The parent cradling a son,
The thief,
The saint,
They'll all be gone.
And when they show
the rows and rows of stones,
We pause.
The hallowed ground
is holding all our pain.
It's hard to breathe.
It's hard to bear
the weight of endings
always in the wings.

And even nature's music
makes its own lament,
Creation groaning
for an earth all bent by sin,
Our sin,
All waiting for the righteous resurrection to begin.

# Hard Truth

It hurts,
This thing that comes to everyone.
Some promise heaven,
Leaving out the Son,
Give the impression
righteousness is easily attained and won.
Some even make it fit their own idolatries,
And dress reality
with different names—
*She passed,*
As if she just moved far away,
*Who lives forever in our hearts.*

We move the cemetery out of sight,
Outside of town,
A rolling lawn fenced off
by groves of trees and climbing walls.
We will forget that death exists,
Until,
Begrudgingly,
We need more real estate.
Some decorate their
green and noble spaces,
Building final resting places
meant to garner sentimental memories
and quiet contemplations,
All for soothing sodden souls
with solid edifices,

Trying hard to reach beyond the great unfathomable
between this life,
And waning dust and bones.
It roughs our soul and breaks our heart.
The miserable and naked truth reveals,
It doesn't matter,
If the memory
is kept within a mausoleum,
Or is lost beneath a row of empty stones
because the names were never known.
We all will die.

# Grief

It startles me,
How easily
an ancient grief,
Quite suddenly,
Can wound again,
Can take a song,
A passing sense of smell,
And capture breath.
Can strike
my unsuspecting heart
with pain remembered.
Here I am again,
Composure fractured,
Lost in sad.
It does not last,
But only heaps a wave
of burdened memory.
It does not keep the teeth
that used to gnaw and chew
upon my bones,
But only takes me
one more time,
To places I once knew
the most alone.

# Numbering

*Here rests,*
The polished marble reads,
*Known but to God.*
And yes,
He knows
what we can only guess.
Too many fields
are sown with death,
The rows of tiny crosses
match the rhythmic flow of stones
like waves.

How painfully
we enter in this world,
How achingly we leave.
The time between
too often short,
Abruptly punctuated starts and stops,
The tenure of our lives
like ticking clocks,
A rush of Now
that never stays.

# The Sting

We're sifting
through old memories,
Passing necklaces and brooches
back and forth,
*This was my mother's,*
*This belonged to Grandma Kelley,*
*Your father gave me this.*
A lifetime,
Now immortalized
through her accessories.
*I remember this,*
*You always looked the best*
*in brown.*
Remembering,
Remembering,
And realizing
she is letting go
one necklace at a time.
*So glad you came,*
She says,
*It's all so providential,*
And we nod together,
Presbyterians to the core.
I'm caught once more.
*Dear* LORD,
I whisper in my head,
*Don't let her stay too long.*
*You know how much*
*she's ready to go home.*

It's been a perfect day.
We've talked,
We painted,
Shared a bit of where we are,
While time is ticking ever forward.
This might be our last time
until we meet again at heaven's door.
I'm trying not to think this way.
I know,
I know,
We all will meet again some day
before the Throne,
And finally be freed
from sin and death.
But now I feel the weight,
The coming loss,
The fact that what has been,
Must go,
Must end.

## The Last Campaign

Death comes to all,
But it is a solitary walk,
A selfish thing
all clamoring to hurry home.
The heart is focused,
Earth,
A fade,
And all of us are left behind.
Those willing to wade up
and touch the edges of the bank,
We only stand on temporal's shore.
Where we are shadows,
She is leaning into light.
Where we are waiting,
She is straining
for that first eternal sight
of Him,
Whom she's been yearning for.

## Body and Soul

When the dust,
The blistering remnants of a thousand upon thousand
    different peoples
and their fading artifacts,
All settle on this ancient world,
And the only archaeologist available
to pick through all that we have been
is God,
Remember,
He has always interacted,
Redirected,
He has been the One with sifting hands,
The One who moved us each in such a way
that everything that we have done,
Has been,
And finally will be,
Has happened by His Holy Will.
And nothing has been left undone.
Our lives,
Our deaths,
Each and every breath,
Each and every moment
dragging through the sorrows,
All the failures,
All the grand successes
we have claimed to be our own,
Particularly the ones we thought had best expressed
    our grand autonomy,

Our own abilities to overcome and worry sin—
Everything we might have named as ours,
Is not our own.
From first created word to calling out the End of Days,
And all the in-between that made humanity,
And gave us memories to sift and weigh,
Belong to Him.

## Grief Comes

Good theology
fills up the cracks and crevices
in this worn,
Leaky house.
It helps
when rain comes hard,
And lengthy shadows lean against the soul,
When sadness
filters in like fog,
The kind
that pulls a person down,
And tries to wrench out weariness.
Good, stout theology
remembers hope,
Remembers promises.
It breathes and thrives
beyond what this old dying universe can see.
It doesn't take the sad away,
But binds it,
Heart and soul,
To grace,
To love,
To what is guaranteed in Christ
for all eternity.

# Separation

She calls it
separation,
Tasting all our human loss,
The ragged longing
in her soul
for one already gone.

We would agree.
For someday soon,
She, too,
Will separate
from all of us.
But she
will also be united
with the Lord,
And reunited
with all those
so long denied.
And that bright
separation,
Separates her soul
from pain,
From sin and death.
And we,
Still waiting,
Separated from her joy,
Will sing our tears,
Will rest in greater promises,
That day she dies.

## Life's Bites

He was an acoustics man.
Knew sound,
Inside and out,
Until he couldn't hear.
I was there,
When he tested both his ears himself.
One side.
There was a pause,
A moment
when reality caught up with hopes.
A gnawing groan,
And all that makes a man,
Was crumbling into deep and whispered sleep.
*Worse than I thought.*
(Was that out loud?)
An almost imperceptible
clenching of his jaw,
A straighter back,
Adjusting from the shrunken shoulders
recently embraced.
And from that place,
He entered
into waiting work.
Somehow the sadness stayed,
But courage
also gained a hold,
And held him in,

As one man
set himself to face
the fight with cancer
he would never win.

## First to Last

Between first breath,
And final breath,
Existence lives.
Our memories
fill up the space.
It seems so short.
Not long enough.
It always is.
We are from earth,
Fighting darkness,
Leaning forward into light,
Waiting on the words and works of God,
Scrambling
to hold all our fragility at bay,
At least as long as breath allows.
So hard to let it go.
It's what we know
until He calls us home.
There is a heaven near,
Not needing air,
Where infinite joy and glory waits,
A greater universe.
And this world drops,
It fades away,
And breathing stops.

## In Honor of Nelson

He has the view,
Up on a hill.
And as far as the eye can see,
It's mountains,
Jumbled,
Spread across the horizon
under an expansive sky.
A nice place to sit nearby
and remember.
You'd like it here,
The conversation starts,
That's why we picked this place.
You were always looking up,
Studying God's green,
His hints of purple, blue and pink,
Those massive waving curtains
hanging from the northern skies.

They're still there,
You know,
And when these colored sails of light
weave and float across the firmament,
We will always think of you,
And whisper to each other,
Just how much you loved the Lord,
And all He made.

# Fear God

## Lost and Wandering

I'm listening to
a known philosopher and teacher
share,
How God is necessary,
Is essential
to the way we need to live.
This man has captured many elements
of good religion,
Insightfully explaining
major points of truth,
Except for one lost,
Vital thought,
One critical,
Forever-binding word—
This teacher knows no father-son relationship,
No running of the Father toward the prodigal,
No knowing you can call on God
at anytime,
In anyplace,
And find Him waiting there.
No Incarnated Son
to touch,
Or feel His healing hand,
And no redemption.
Only Us,
The ones who,
Somehow,

Must acknowledge God,
Yet crawl ourselves out from
our own primordial sin,
And rise to meet this Necessary Spirit
somewhere in the air.

## A Fork in the Road

One man turned his face
from God,
But still God gifted him—
A generous heart,
An eager, curious mind,
Abilities
that gave him graces in invention
and in leadership—
All this world could offer
came his way.
He gained a caring wife,
A family,
A lovely home,
And opportunities
becoming more important
than the people in his life.
He knew somehow
that time was flying by,
That someday time would capture everything,
And take it all away,
The ticking second hand
unwinding every corner of his life.
And yet,
He kept on gathering,
Accumulating everything he could,
So sure he'd have the time one day to play,
To finally sit down and read that book,
To tell his children stories of his youth.
The only thing that mattered most

was capturing all that he could.
He never asked for God,
He never would.
Religion in his mind,
A whim, a chasing after wind.
He had so much.
This world was all there was for him.
And just before he died,
Shocked to his very core,
To have his padded universe wrapped up so soon
and packed away,
He thought,
*He had so much.*
*It's not enough!*
*It's not enough!*
And in his final breath,
As all he worked hard to achieve returned to dust
before his fading eyes,
He cried.

One man turned his face
toward God,
And God reached down
and gifted him—
A generous heart,
An eager, curious mind,
A busy life.
Working hard,
From sunrise
on into the night,
He kept a job he struggled with.
The work allowed him time at home,
Time for worship Sunday morning,
Time to join with neighbors on his street.

Well out of reach:
Accumulating stuff,
Competing for the bigger pay,
The cushy office,
Nameplate on the door.

Second-hand and bartering
a better match,
A fair exchange for time with friends he greeted on his daily walks.
Always very keen on time,
It goes too fast,
It didn't even slow when he was savoring the time he had.
Time,
Time,
Always time,
The ticking second hand
unwinding every corner of his life,
And yet,
He soldiered on,
Retiring a week or two
before his death,
His loving family
(kindly wife,
And noisy brood)
Left standing by his bed.
The only thing that mattered most—
The hour-by-hour relationship with God,
That love between the Father and adopted son,
Had carried him,
Had made his work,
His life,
His family,
His neighborhood,
A place where grace had generously abounded all his days.
*He had so much,*

A thankful, fleeting thought
before his final breath.
And then he left this world
and all it possibly could have ever offered him,
For better worlds,
For greater graces,
God Himself,
The greatest gift was ready to be found.

## Let Me Hide Myself in Thee

I wonder how it really was inside,
When Sheila whipped through
old age,
While the cancer grew,
When she trudged forward
to the walker stage
for just one week,
Instead of months or years.
What arguments
between the penitent and God,
Went on,
As speeding limitations
swallowed up autonomy,
And snatched her sense of independence
out from under her?
It's difficult enough,
When ordinary aging,
Makes the changing,
As the losses flow,
A daily challenge
to a body forced to recognize
a host of growing weaknesses,
The failures of a system breaking down,
When heart and soul
still only see a younger self.
How difficult to come to terms,
And to embrace what God ordains,
What human frailty sustains,
When every door is closing one by one,

And being sanctified,
At last encompasses the end of life.
My sister took the tour
at forty-four.

It doesn't matter
if we stumble through the tour
in weeks or years.
It feels the same—
The loss,
The recognizing just how short
our travels are,
How simple our priorities,
How central to be found in Christ
as we are now devoured by our earthly pain,
How focusing on Holy Providence,
When suffering,
Reminds us of God's promises infused in us,
His daily comfort leading and encouraging.
Through every dreadful, struggling day,
Divine untangling,
His laboring on our behalf,
Is separating will and heart from earthly loves,
Preparing us for final gain.

# The Wonder of the Cross

The pilgrim sheds
a bucket–load of carelessness,
And all the tattered remnants
fall like ash
upon his neighbors,
All of those this creature meets.
Why would anyone
so easily
spread shadows?
Gift disorder,
Dust the world
with agonies and sorrows in their wake,
Let peace melt down
and honor break?

The neighbors claim they feel the loss,
And cast the blame,
But each and every one,
Is one who sheds,
And each and every one
encapsulates the cost.
Each person carries
deep within his heart
the ruthlessness no person ever wants to show,
But always wears.
Such darkness digs the soul down into dirt,
And trying to escape,
Just further scrapes the earth.
Such futile, empty struggles bury hope and breed despair.

*We are the stumbling,*
*The restlessness of shattered grace,*
*They are,*
*We are,*
*We were,*
*And none of us can wrestle free.*
*We would be lost,*
The pilgrim says and nods his head,
*Except the wonder of the Cross.*

*Why would our God*
*take on Himself*
*the cosmic torments of abandonment,*
The pilgrim cries,
*Why must He suffer for my hard deceit?*

Except to make a peace.
Except to offer up His blood,
The only disinfectant
able to expunge the sin.
Except to crush the Serpent's head.
Except to squeeze the darkness out of life,
And raise the dead.

The Cross lifts up a vacant face,
And gives back sight.
The Cross blows life,
Like mighty wind,
Into a shriven soul,
And there is breath.
The Cross claws off
the scabs and scars of shame,
The weight of guilt and sin,
And skin and bones
can finally reach out beyond the grave,

Beyond the dirt,
And conquer death.
The Cross absorbs
a bucket-load of carelessness,
And all the tattered remnants
burn away like ash.

*I would be cringing vapors,*
*Only aching, wasted breaths,*
*A passing cough,*
*I would be lost,*
The pilgrim soul repeats,
And revels that his Maker wore this sinner's condemnation,
Propitiation savoring the mercy seat.
*I would be lost,*
*Except the wonder of the Cross.*

## Under the Blood

Church
is not an echo chamber
for religious conversations,
Only rituals and rites
practiced every week
like clock-work,
Insulated
from the piercing
of the sacred Word,
The penetrating Sword,
Dividing selfishness and secret thoughts,
The "everything is love to me,"
That worldlings wear,
From dreadful Holiness,
And what the Cross
was called to bear.

We need the graver
views of wrath
and sacrifice,
The need for blood,
The strength of Truth,
The single clarity of Hope
that only Righteousness
alone can share.

## Rebuttal

God says,
Forgive.
Not seven times,
But seventy times seven.
And I am Peter,
Trying to parse out a paltry kindness
I don't even want to give.
God says,
Rejoice as you share suffering with Christ.
Expect the sufferings to rumble
all the way through out your life,
To carve out scars
that build an understanding heart,
A tensile strength,
A keen humility.
My burdens always offer sacred comfort,
Grace that heals the woundings
left by strife.

But Lord,
I start again,
Expecting sympathy.
A sliver of entitlement
is itching to be free.
Excuses justifying my unhappiness,
My disappointment,
Waiting to become
my next crusade.

*Apart from me,*
God gently says,
*You could have been
the same as him.
Did you forget
it was my Son that you betrayed?*

## Holy Food

He boldly states
He is the Living Bread,
And those who come to Him,
And who believe,
Will never hunger,
Never thirst.
He's speaking of His death, of course,
His bloody sacrifice
as God's true manna.
*What is it*
is fast becoming,
*What it is*
*that satisfies the payment*
*for our sin.*
It's hard to take this in,
For when He metaphors this Truth—
Unless you eat my body,
Drink my blood—
*These are hard words,*
*And who can hear or understand?*
They say,
And many walk away.
They will no longer
follow Him.

This world is harder still,
And we will not survive
without a better food.

There is no refuge
for the hungry soul,
No holy eating
where our hearts are truly fed,
No nourishment
for flesh and bone,
That sates like Living Bread.

# Fidget

He quarreled with God
for many years,
Not wanting to give up
his right to choose,
To make a name,
And show the world and God
just who he was.
He didn't give up church,
Or Bible study Wednesday nights.
He loved the Lord,
Just wanted to be part of naming terms
in his engagement with divinity.
He filled his life with memories,
Experiences,
He never truly settled down.
So much to learn
and even more to do.
To him,
A restless spirit was his virtue,
Something urging him
to overwhelm and conquer,
Push against the edges,
All the ceilings
that could hold him back,
Or might prevent the fullest life,
And all its rich entanglements.
And yet,
There was no rest.

He tried to fit it in—
A Christmas cruise,
Membership to popular amusement parks,
Evenings at the pub
for beer and games of darts—
All lovely fun
that left him tired,
Not refreshed.
There was no rest.

And even if he felt
like there were moments he relaxed,
It didn't last.
His restlessness went on and on,
Its hunger eating up
the very passions hurrying his heart.
If only there was time enough
to do it all.

And then there wasn't.

Time unwinding,
Sucked up all the air
to where he had to stop,
To listen for that still small voice,
The One that had been always there,
The God
he'd tried to keep
just slightly out of reach.
This God was reaching out,
And waiting to be heard,
The only One who truly understood
the restless yearning that had dogged this man from year to year,
But never really gained what he was sure he had deserved.
(Forgetting he deserved to be denied,

Destroyed
without the Christ who kept him near.)
Amazingly,
Grace had decreed that
that which he desired most
was God,
The God who was Himself
the rest
that this man's roaming heart required.

## Promises

When life has offered instability,
*I'll keep you safe*
can grab a heart.
When there has never been enough
of love,
Of grace,
Of food or shelter,
*Free*
can eagerly embrace a soul
and hold it fast.
And greedy
doesn't sound so bad
when souls are starving,
Wasting,
Gnawing into needs
connected to our
private loathing,
All our hating being frail,
For being finite in a universe
that needs someone
whose promises
can never fail,
And always last.
We are a world
with people saying one thing,
Promising to be there
when it counts,
And suddenly,
They have too much to do,

They would be there
if only you had asked another day.
They say they are your friends,
And wish they had the time.
And even death
can callously collide
with expectations,
One hand offering
a hopeful promise,
Then the other
taking hope,
Stability,
And love away.
Into this fractured daily life,
God says
*He goes before us,*
*He will never leave us,*
*Nor forsake His own.*
He says
*He has already*
*overcome this world.*
This world,
The one that overwhelms us everyday.
And we are called to walk by faith,
Not only worship if it fits
our present circumstance,
But constantly,
Remembering that
He will do
just what He says,
And only He can make it true.

## This is the Day

Every morning
I wake up,
And think,
This is the day
the LORD has made,
And then
I walk the dog,
And think about
a million different worries,
Daily lists,
Instead of Him.
Even if the Scriptures
from the morning,
Stay inside my head,
No matter where my thoughts have been,
My heart's a wandering thing.
This is the day
the LORD has made,
I say again.

Today,
I promptly fall
when going through the motions
of an ordinary day,
And end up getting x-rays.
Suddenly
I am a fractured foot,
An awkward,
Painful stance,

Distorted place,
With searing pain
that follows me
from room to room.
*Whate'er my God*
*ordains is right,*
Comes singing in my head.
Yes, yes,
I do believe in Providence,
In Sacred Will,
But still,
I wonder why
He felt the need to wound.
It does not feel
like sanctifying grace,
It feels like aggravations,
Limitations,
Getting old and fragile
much too fast.
This is the day the Lord has made.

## Rough Seas

When strife breaks through,
And wounds me once again,
And I am ready to move on,
To drop my troubles off,
Donate them,
Walk away and don't look back,
I find I'm flailing,
Lost in roiling storms.
They're here!
They're here!
They ride me,
Follow me
no matter what I do.
I would let them go,
But He would have
me hold my troubles tighter still.
And like a tired,
Tattered boat in raging seas
that pins me fast
against a shuttering pier,
I'm shaking here.
It's hard to hear you LORD, right now.

I'm trying to hang on
in spite of water in the bilge,
In spite of slapping waves,
In spite of stinging salt.

I thought I understood
how far
that You would go
to bring me safely home.
I find there's more to learn,
More to struggle through.
He wants me leaning
straight into the wind.
He wants me leaning harder into Him,
Demanding everything,
Providing anchor
in my darkest corners,
Places where my heart
is lost in fears,
Providing refuge,
Just enough
to keep me near to shore,
Just enough
to keep my battered soul afloat,
Just enough
to hold me close,
When waves roll in
and fling me hard against the rocks.
And I keep thinking,
Any moment I'll be lost,
But He is never letting go.
And so,
This is my worship,
Leaning hard into the wind,
And into Him.
Feeling helpless once again.

## Sacred Guardians

So grateful
there are prophets speaking,
Men and women,
Standing up for Truth
amidst the soothing speech
of dark invention,
Dangerous libel
ever snaking into thoughts and vulnerable affections.
Only those who wield the Word
can conquer dragons,
Stopping mouths of monsters
eating wayward hearts,
And spitting out the souls.

So thankful
there are people
dwelling here among the fallen,
And the suffering,
Befriending faithfulness,
And lending generously
as God has done before for them.
God's children are not refuse
of another's goals,
But fragrant offerings of grace,
A sacrifice of praise,
The hands and feet of peace,
Upending battles raging
deep within the night.

They move with patience
as they fight,
And do not fret,
Entrusting their own lives
to Him who judges justly,
Trusting in the Lord,
And doing right.

# Letting Go

Sometimes You ask
a lot of us.
I know,
I know,
It's for our good,
And You are glorified.
But so much suffering—
It doesn't feel so righteous
when the cancer cuts
and mutilates,
The cures too often,
Seem much worse
than raging,
Growing cells.
It seems unkind
when aging robs the body.
Dignity is always first to go,
Then independence follows,
Sometimes furious and swift,
Sometimes slow.

This peeling away
of humanity
for the sake of the Cross,
For the sake of the soul—
Some days it is a bitter war,
A fight
between my pride,
My own desire for grand autonomy

against a greater resting
in such tender graces
I can barely comprehend or know.
This dying to ourselves
takes everything,
My letting go of all the little gods
I hold and covet carefully.
By inches,
I am called to lose it all.
And You,
Becoming
lowest of the low,
A servant to an angry,
Arrogant world,
You,
The brightest,
Wisest,
Most obedient in Love,
Becoming strangely most obedient in death.
How terrible are we
in all our sin.
How terrible is Love,
That only sacrificial death could draw us in.
How marvelous,
The dreadful tearing
of our deepest enmity,
To set us free.

## Discerning Grace

So difficult to know the truth
down here,
To separate the facts
from fiction,
Disinformation clawing,
Scarring
sacred soul,
Ripping
truth from hearts,
Confusing minds,
And dulling ears to hear
what Righteousness is whispering,
Reality is shouting
to a world that stumbles—
Lost and blind.

How can they believe in Him
of whom they've never heard?
Where are the hands and feet
that speak the Truth
with kindness and compassion?
Where are the mouths that preach?

It is not politics we need.
It is not social justice warriors,
But God's hard justice satisfied
in Jesus Christ,
That heals the soul,

That speaks His mercy through His Word,
That clears the fog,
That separates the liar
from his prey,
That chases out confusion,
Redirecting hearts
toward blessing,
And toward grace.

## To My Granddaughter

There is a wise old woman
growing deep inside of you,
And I am catching glimpses
of her,
In your youthful face.
For you,
Like Jacob
Felt God's hand of loving providence
collide with flesh,
As you were wrestling in heart and soul.
And now you live,
A woman touched by Him,
A circumstance of grace
that He will use
to make you whole,
Will take the troubles,
And the sorrows
that this life has doled,
And mold them into excellencies of faith,
That will endure.
I see you here,
Already reaching to the sky
with humbleness and prayer.
And when I do,
I see the wise old woman there.

# The Last Battle

She's reaching
the end of all her years.
*There are so many,*
She says,
And remembering
stills warms her heart.
But the sweet now runs
along with sad,
There is a bite
to ordinary days.
Vexation rends the pleasure off,
And leaves the tears.
Creaking joints,
Aching back,
Hands don't grasp
the way they should.
She knows just what
she needs to do,
But ancient parts
refuse to play,
And won't repent,
While muscles hate to follow
all the strict instructions
that her tired mind has sent.
She's fighting back,
She plans to mend.
Too late, I think.
The world rolls on,
Her world would stop.

She'd run away,
If only painful knees and feet
could tackle stairs,
And manage street.

Her LORD says,
Stay.
Read.
Rest.
This is the place
I've called you to.

It's hard to do.

This is the season age relents
from rush and roam.
This room,
This space,
This energy,
Is all about preparing her
for coming home.

## The Latest Race

She's running with endurance.
*Every day,*
She says.
It doesn't feel that way.
It feels like pain,
Like loss,
A constant cross to bear,
Where limitations grow,
Encroach
on all her strength.
Some days she's fighting back
with little gain.
Some days,
Too tired even to complain.
She'd run away,
But being seventy-five
does not leave much room for grand,
Successful forays,
As her body functions
less like fire,
And more like fog and rain.

Today she read,
*I've fought the fight,*
*I've finished the race,*
*I've kept the faith.*
The Holy Spirit,
Comforting a weary heart,

Reminds her
He's been making sacred room
to give her rest.
She's shaking off this life,
So that the things
that cannot ever be undone,
Unmade,
Cannot be shaken,
All these things,
For always will remain,
And she is truly blest.

# A Soliloquy of Faith

Be aware.
Those thousand natural shocks
are there
to carve compassion,
Resurrect the soul,
Unleash the grit
that builds with steady providence,
A long endurance,
Underpinning all our trials,
All of our despair.
Because He did return
from traveling that
undiscovered country,
We no longer only bear our ills,
But find a greater courage,
Capture blazing hope,
Transforming hearts,
And making whole.

# Resting

Here I am again,
Resting here
between Your shoulders.
Strength has fled.
My heart feels crooked,
Bent,
So difficult to understand the way.
I cannot find the path.
The weight of life
has burdened hope,
And all I see is what I lack.
And I am thinking,
*Just keep walking,*
*Forward,*
*Moving forward.*
How glad I am,
Instead,
To find I'm resting here
upon Your back.
Without Your carrying,
My soul is spent.

## I Am Unraveled

Inclined to wander
sounds too tame,
Too mundane.
I am unraveled,
Searching in the wrong directions,
Getting tangled up
in life's concerns,
Unsettled by the struggles,
Underwriting all my energies
with various solutions:
Standing still,
Not doing anything of consequence,
Pressing forward,
Hoping strength
(I haven't got)
will see me through.

*Feeling far away from you,*
*Oh God,*
*And here I am awake*
*and plotting in the dark.*
*I'm stuck.*
*I'm floored.*
I know He's here.
Why can't I see salvation in the LORD?

## Providence

Pouring milk into a bowl,
Stirring pots up on the stove,
Wiping one more nose,
That's ordinary
gracious love from day to day.

Sitting with an anxious friend,
Really hearing
that old story everybody knows,
From beginning to the end.
That's ordinary
gracious love from day to day.

Getting up at five
to hit the road
before the traffic blocks the way,
Working in a cubicle
with spreadsheets,
Deadlines once again,
Because someone depends on
you to bring the money in,
That's ordinary
gracious love from day to day.

It may not feel that gracious,
Or that loving day to day,
The disappointments,
Lack of sleep,

The unplanned plumbing
keeping tensions in the air,
The boss who doesn't understand,
The traffic makes us late,
A child is sick
and cries all night,
And each of us
goes limping on.
What can we do?

Dear God,
We cry,
We wish this life
could be less messy,
More in tune.
Please, Father,
Get us through.

And there He is,
In every single moment,
Somehow weaving
all our struggles,
All our failures,
All our ordinary,
Into blessings—
Some so painful,
That they pierce our very soul,
And others,
Gentler,
Whisper kindness,
Care,
So beautiful,
It makes us whole.

We might have missed His providence,
Except He made us stop and notice,
In our dull and maddening ordinary,
Mixed up with the troubles
that we wear.

*Come and see*
*such grand,*
*Extraordinary love from day to day,*
He says to us,
*Come meet My ordinary.*
*You'll never be alone.*
*I'm always there.*

## Last Days

She's eating up
as many moments
as she can.
No time for sleep.
There will be
opportunities for that,
When she lays down this world
for good,
For brighter,
New accommodations,
Gaining that address
on every Christian's bucket list.

This may be
her last chance
to pass on precious wisdom
gained from pain,
From loss,
From leaning into Christ,
When nothing else
could possibly support,
And she is living it
before us all,
Shuffling around her aching parts.

Old days,
And all their energies,
Have secreted away
sometime ago,
To leave behind a sacred core,
Where she still soldiers on,
The essence of heroic hearts.

## God With Us

He is a burning bush.
God With Us
means take off both your shoes.
Back up!
This is a holy place.

He is the blood upon the door,
The crimson marks that claim
a people for Himself,
That stand between our death
and His.
God With Us
means huddled,
Helpless people,
Waiting,
While death's angel
crouches at the gates
to take a woman's son.
God With Us
means you are His.
It is His blood,
His death that
covers yours.

He is a rock,
Struck hard
to save a thirsty,
Quarreling people,
Never satisfied.

God With Us
means water,
Means rebuke,
Means finding out
that testing draws the worst from us,
The best from Him.
We might have died,
Except He bore our Meribah,
Our hubris,
All our stingy,
Miserly ungratefulness,
And bids us drink.
This is a holy place.

He is a pillar of fire by night,
A cloud by day,
And tired,
Frightened people
find their way
by walking through the waters,
Not around.
God With Us
means passing through,
Walking confidently,
Knowing that the Lord
will fight for you.
This is a holy place.

He is a blazing fire,
Furious lightening
thundering through turbulent clouds.
The mountain trembles,
Wreathed in burning smoke.
Can any bear such glory
in His coming?

All who see know
God With Us
means be afraid,
Bow down before such holiness,
Or you will die.
Stay clear!
Don't get too close.
This is a holy place.

He is
a baby in a woman's womb.
God With Us
means being born into obscurity,
No matter that the royal shock troops
shouted out His coming.
Who believes what shepherds say?
What good has ever come from Nazareth?
And who is anyone in quiet Bethlehem today?
God With Us
accepts a sacred solidarity
with lost and broken souls.
For all of us could be forgotten,
Cast aside—
For we are liars,
Foolish,
Faithless,
Heartless,
Insolent and boastful people.
Yet such holiness and grace
allows a human hand to touch and kiss His face,
And not be burned.
God With Us
means reaching down
to rescue those who need Him most.

God With Us
means being wrapped
in cloths for infancy,
And wrapped again in death,
His body in a borrowed tomb.
God With Us
means carrying the worst of us,
And giving back to us His best.
*Come drink,*
*Come eat,*
He says.
*Come know my rest.*
This is a holy place.

# A Pleasing Aroma

## I Didn't Know How Hungry I Was

When beauty passes by,
I cry.
It cuts me open,
Soul exposed,
Revealing such a yearning
from the heart,
To savor all the goodness
while it lasts.
If only I were able
to sustain
the elegance,
The tenderness,
The Light,
The peace.
Dear Lord,
It's You I want,
It's You I need.
And this sweet moment
gently offers grace,
A pale reflection of Yourself,
And now,
It's gone,
And I,
Bereft,
Hold on.
Dear Lord,
I had forgotten
just how hungry I have been
to seek Your face.

## A Pleasing Aroma

Can anybody tell
that you've been
sprinkled with the blood?
I know it doesn't show.
There is no slaughter,
With its cloying,
Putrid odors,
No ordinary sense that death,
His death,
For our decay,
Was necessary
to expunge the debt.
But here and there,
Amazing fragrance,
Sweet aromas of forgiveness,
Scents of kindness and compassion,
Spices waiting in
the possibility of hope,
Something unbelievers,
Searchers,
Can't quite put their fingers on,
But there it is.
And as we drive the freeway,
Organize our produce
on the cashier's long conveyor belt,
Interact with neighbors,
Every place we go,
The breeze of peace
is floating near.

Everywhere,
Its sacred smells exuding holy grace,
Quite often in our stumbling,
In our most awkward moments,
In our daily struggles,
Despite our fears and doubts.
In everything,
The sacred blood
that has been sprinkled
on our heads,
Most fervently
is overcoming,
Holy Life invading darkness and despair.
For Christ and all His promises,
Are filling up the air.

# Who But God

Who but God
could make amends,
Could wear our skin and bones
without the wreckage
weaving in and out of cells.
Who but God
could truly carry weight
we thought we owned,
The glory we desired,
Glory only passing through us,
Sacred parts no longer welcomed
as our hearts abandoned light.
For we are ghosts,
Preferring to embrace the night.

Who but God,
The One most solid,
He who was most whole,
Would let us
pummel Him with angry fists,
Would let us
vent against our emptiness
and our despair,
Our restlessness,
Our cold desires for the tainted things,
Our arrogance and our hypocrisy,
By killing Him.

How could we understand
that this one man would eat our enmity,
Our unforgiving, storming hearts,
Would swallow our depravity and pain.
Would blow apart the universe,
And snatch it back again?

Who but God?

## And Then They Sang

And they sang on
in perfect harmony,
Just twenty voices
blending perfectly.
It was as if
the highest contemplations,
Suddenly were given shape
and sound,
A unity of notes,
A melody so tight,
So gracefully profound,
That every single thought expressed
a gentleness,
A kindness
permeating skin and soul
with light,
With promises of spring,
And all of my remembering
was turned to hope.
How bright!
How comforting can music be!
And how endearingly are
gracious hearts
that sing away the dark,
When bones are sad,
When earth is weight,

And life,
Too many times,
Resounds with knells,
And mournful bells
instead of promises,
When all the elements of sorrow
clammer to be found,
An echo rumbling,
Reverberating
on and on,
An endless clang.
I had forgotten
(for a moment)
just how wonderful you are,
Oh Lord,
And then they sang.

## Sight Unseen

Some people
serve as hands and feet
for God's own sacred universe,
Not knowing
that their slivers of His Truth,
Are speaking Grace.
They don't believe
that God exists,
But there they are,
Dispensing Him by handfuls,
Unaware.
They are partaking in His Holy Will,
Expressing beauty,
Mercy,
Love,
God's character displayed
in those who would
refuse Him to His face.

## Stones Speak

What shimmering light is music,
Spilling all it glories over hearts
with warmth,
With zest!
Such sounds
bring beauty into hearing,
Possibilities of hope,
Of honor,
And of justice,
Rising like a fire deep within our souls.
*Surely here,*
We say,
*Has beauty spoken best.*

And yet,
The edifices guarding
all the sweetest melodies,
The head,
The heart,
The ears and voice,
Each layered brick and concrete shell
are only grand memorials
to what we tell
about what we have done.

How often is the ancient psalter sung,
Completely freed from reconciliation,
Freed from true contrition,

Separated from the righteous words
we gloriously sing,
Remembering what we have never known.
How difficult it is to understand
why many You have gifted
with the grace to sing Your praises—
These will never know You,
Never comprehend the mystery and majesty of You,
Will live for their own harmonies,
Will love themselves.

And You,
The least.

Still,
Stoney hearts will speak.
They sing aloud of You,
And of Your truth.
*Surely here,*
You say.
*That even if Your children would be silent,*
*Even then,*
*The very stones would cry out,*
*Calling after You.*

And so they do.

## God's Re-creation

We who are God's people,
We who have been gifted holy DNA,
Are being changed.
Our temperaments,
Our habits altered
and updated,
Re-created,
Even as we live
in this constructing / deconstructing world.
No matter what is shaped,
Or scraped,
Or molded over skin and bone—
Such earthly framing does not last.

But what is righteous,
Sacred parts re-writing nature's code,
Is now reviving
every cell,
Each and every molecule,
Even now the whole of holy being seared
into our very soul.
And we,
Never far from trial,
Sometimes fighting with despair,
Always here and now afflicted,
At this very moment,
Are becoming something rare,
Made to bear
the weight of God's eternal glory.

## The Tall Man

He's always had
the straightest back,
A military stance
acquired early in his life.
But recently,
I notice that
the back is bending,
Leaning forward,
Gravity.
And all the weight of ordinary strife,
Is slowly drawing
this man's face toward earth.

It's not the spirit
of the man.
His heart and focus still stand tall.
But all
the years and years
of carrying another's pain
inside his own,
A life of well-lived kindnesses and caring,
Love itself
can make the bends.
Where comforting and holding
tends to build a crooked
into straight.
And knowing loss and sorrow,
All the weight of stumbling,

Can rearrange the carriage
of a man,
When Grace is poured,
As he accepts
the privilege and burden borne
in doing justice,
Loving mercy,
Walking humbly
with the Lord.

# Rescue

There is a mourning
for an only Son,
And that bleak keening day
is bitter
Tasting of abandonment
so dark
So full of sorrowing,
That even hope
is ground down into dust,
And trust,
Reduced to whispers,
Wavers,
Wonders if there could be
any glorious days ahead.
But the Temple curtains
tear from top to bottom,
Many of the dead
are now alive,
And walking into town.
This miracle profound!
O death, here is your sting!
It's here!
It's here!
The Son has taken it away,
And left me standing,
Hoping,
Praying once again
while blossoms still are blown like snow,

And this bowed down creation
still is dragging by.
I see the mourners still
are walking up and down
and moaning,
Saying,
*This world soon will go,*
*And there is no eternity,*
The pitchers shatter here and there,
And bowls are broken,
Dust returns to earth,
But I am free!
I will be going home!
I'm free!
O death, where is your victory!

# One Night

They're back
out in the field,
Keeping watch
over flocks by night.
At least one
should be guarding sheep,
But who can sleep?
Darkness mixed
with bleating flocks,
The same old,
Same old,
Counting lambs,
Alert for nature's predators,
The nightly wonder
of a field of stars,
And conversations hushed,
With talks of market business,
Separating blemished
from unblemished,
The Feast of Passover is coming,
Do we have enough for sacrifice?

But not tonight.
The same old,
Same old—
Gone in one huge flash
of brilliant light,
As sacred
breaks the sky,

And hides the stars,
To bring the message
all humanity has waited for.

For centuries,
Good neighbors nodded to each other,
Asking,
Hoping,
Is this the day Messiah comes?

This is the day.
And why have we been honored
with the news?
Been shattered with the shouting chorus
of His entourage,
A thundering praise
that overwhelms both man and beast?

They run
to meet such wonder—
Wrapped in swaddling cloths,
And lying in a manger—
Who can comprehend?
Who can balance words
of priests and kings
with what we've seen and heard?
Who will listen to the likes of us?

They will obey and worship Him,
And rush to share
this ancient promise suddenly
becoming Truth.
Who could understand, or fathom
such realities,
So deep?

They're back
out in the field,
Keeping watch
over flocks by night.
At least one
should be guarding sheep,
But who can sleep?

## My Soul Waits for the Lord

*I wait for the* Lord,
Seems like forever
when you're waiting for
the Son to come.
And then the last three
years of thirty-three
come roaring past,
The culmination of a promise made
to nascent man,
When everything was faltering,
And what had been
so fresh,
Was absolutely spoiled,
Judgment crackling in the air.

And every son
who follows Seth,
A mother hopes and prays,
*Is this the One?*
And every father groans
to see his progeny
become instead,
Just like his dad,
Incapable of undermining sin,
Too many times,
More friend than foe
with human woe.

Each generation
looking for a sign,
Those ancient words repeated over time.
*Is this the One?*

*I wait for the* LORD.
*My soul waits.*
Year by year,
King by king,
Through exile and return,
A people conquered yet again,
Not just by outside armies,
But their very hearts.
It seems forever just the same,
No end.
And still,
Redemption is a lamb,
A goat,
A dove.
But nothing satisfies
the soul of Man,
The desperate longing,
Yearning for a better world,
A better son.

*I wait for the* LORD.
*My soul waits,*
*And in His word I hope.*
Then suddenly,
All time begins unwinding Adam's curse
as shepherds hear
Good News proclaimed,
And Simeon,

Who holds the promised Son
in waiting arms,
Will speak Messiah named.
*Now let your servant here*
*depart in peace.*
*My eyes have seen Salvation.*

*My soul waits for the* LORD
*more than watchmen for the morning.*
Come and see.
This is the One.
This Sacred Son
is walking Israel's dusty roads,
To teach,
To touch,
To tabernacle
with His stiff-necked people,
Those who need Him most,
And love Him least.
His ministry will take Him
through a dark and barren place,
Full of furious religiosity,
But little grace.
It is a messy,
Necessary,
Painful calling to endure,
Restoring members of
the human race.
Three years,
He has been generously
redeeming sight,
Unlocking crumpled legs,
Unbending hearts and egos,
Making straight a host of crooked backs,

Forgiving sin,
Always dismantling our misery and hate.
Only He can claim what wrath requires
to unlock our fate.
This job takes blood,
And He will give it all.

Seems like forever
when you're waiting for
the Son to come.
And then the last three aching,
Yet triumphant years,
Come roaring past.
Come and see such Grace poured out,
Come know His glorious gift of freedom
sprinkled on a waiting world!
*O Israel, hope in the* LORD*!*
*For with the* LORD *there is steadfast love,*
*And with Him is plentiful redemption.*
Come. He will redeem.

## Final Thoughts

How much do we rely
upon our dreams,
And our desire?
Instead of building up ourselves
in holy faith,
Instead of running eager fingers
over pages of His Word,
(What glorious translation of His truth is waiting there!)
Forgetting how He
snatched us from the fire?
There are no deeds
He has not seen,
No secret things
He does not know—
Our stumbling,
The weariness of soul in man.
And yet He loves.
We would do better fearing God,
And keeping His commands.